TO

....

FROM

....

DATE

....

GOD'S WISDOM® FOR
THE GRADUATE

CLASS OF
2023

An Imprint of Thomas Nelson Publishers

THOMAS NELSON
Since 1798

CONTENTS

INTRODUCTION

You graduated! Congratulations! All your efforts and persistence have led to a noteworthy achievement well worth celebrating! Now you're ready to begin your journey toward a successful life.

But what exactly is success, and how do you find it? So many people offer opinions. These days we can read about success in how-to books, listen to podcasts to gain tips, and witness inspiring examples in all fields of endeavor. Everyone wants to know the formula for brilliant accomplishment.

The Christian, however, wants to experience success *with eternal value.* And the best contributor to that kind of success is wisdom, specifically God's. In His Word, God offers guidelines by which we should live. When we follow them, we will experience the success He has for us—the kind that matters and lasts.

When you need wisdom, seek the Lord's face, and let Him be your guide. He wants the best for you, and in Him "are hidden all the treasures of wisdom and knowledge" (Colossians 2:3). God's wisdom will help you live a life of Christlike service and glorify Him in all you do. And that truly is success.

IT'S NOT A SOLO JOURNEY

There's nothing like a cap and gown to get a person thinking about the future!

Despite the unknowns, what lies ahead for you is exciting—even if you wonder how you'll navigate the waters. As you consider the future, rest assured that you won't be going it alone.

We know this because one name for Jesus is *Emmanuel*, which means "God with us." Jesus is with you today, and He promises to be with you tomorrow and every day after that.

God is available to us via His Word. In the Bible's pages, you'll find God's guidance for any situation that comes your way and all the decisions and troubles you will face. "If any of you lacks wisdom, let him ask of God . . . and it will be given to him" (James 1:5).

And finally, He draws close to us in prayer: "The Lord is near to all who call upon Him, to all who call upon Him in truth" (Psalm 145:18).

With gifts like prayer, wisdom, and Jesus' very presence, your life is never a solo journey. What a comfort!

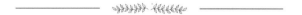

"I am with you always, even to the end of the age."

MATTHEW 28:20

The Lord is my shepherd;
I shall not want.
He makes me to lie down in green pastures;
He leads me beside the still waters.
He restores my soul.

PSALM 23:1-3

And He said, "My Presence will go with you, and I will give you rest."

EXODUS 33:14

Surely goodness and mercy shall follow me
All the days of my life;
And I will dwell in the house of the LORD
Forever.

PSALM 23:6

WHEN CHALLENGES COME, LOOK TO GOD

When we walk with God, He enables us to deal with such challenges as final exams, new roommates, homesickness, unreasonable deadlines, and demanding bosses. When relying on God's Spirit, we turn over to Him our worries and fears—and leave them with Him.

Free of those burdens, we more easily succeed in honoring God in the way we live. Yet we often use the words *can't* and *won't* when thinking about our problems. God offers both solutions and confidence, as well as an eternal perspective: "Count it all joy when you fall into various trials, knowing that the testing of your faith produces patience. But let patience have its perfect work" (James 1:2–4).

When challenges come, and they will, look

to God. Remind yourself that He is with you, remember His faithfulness to you in the past, and pray for the blessing of His guidance, strength, and wisdom.

Be anxious for nothing, but in everything by prayer and supplication, with thanksgiving, let your requests be made known to God; and the peace of God, which surpasses all understanding, will guard your hearts and minds through Christ Jesus.

PHILIPPIANS 4:6–7

Cast your burden on the LORD,
And He shall sustain you;
He shall never permit the righteous to be
   moved.

PSALM 55:22

"Do not worry about your life. . . . Look at the birds of the air, for they neither sow nor reap nor gather into barns; yet your heavenly Father feeds them. Are you not of more value than they?"

MATTHEW 6:25-26

GOD-GIVEN HOPE

G od knows you. He knows where you are—physically, emotionally, and spiritually. He sees you. He loves you. He longs to show you His love by His actions and to guide you throughout your life.

But Satan, the enemy of your soul, wants you to believe that God is uninterested in you, that people who follow Him flounder and fail, and that a loving God would prevent pain, injustice, and loss.

God, however, knows the crossroads you face, and He wants you to know you can trust Him as you step forward in faith. After all, "our help is in the name of the LORD, who made heaven and earth" (Psalm 124:8). You can't top that!

God has good plans for you. Choose to believe that truth, and then rest in that hope.

"I know the thoughts that I think toward
you," says the Lord, "thoughts of peace and
not of evil, to give you a future and a hope."

JEREMIAH 29:11

The Lord is my strength and my shield;
My heart trusted in Him, and I am helped;
Therefore my heart greatly rejoices,
And with my song I will praise Him.

PSALM 28:7

You have been my help,
Therefore in the shadow of Your wings I will
rejoice.

PSALM 63:7

The Lord will give strength to His people;
The Lord will bless His people with peace.

PSALM 29:11

NO FEAR OF FAILURE

*F**ear* and *failure* are two words that often go together. Either one can lead to the other.

But because our sovereign God reigns, fear and failure don't need to threaten us. Clare Boothe Luce said, "There are no hopeless situations; there are only men who have grown hopeless about them." When problems seem unsolvable, look to God, and you might see those tough circumstances as exhilarating challenges. God may help you identify invisible exits in what looks like a dead-end street.

When the Syrians attacked Israel, Elisha's servant was terrified by the enemy's strength. But when Elisha prayed, the young man saw that "the mountain was full of horses and chariots of fire" (2 Kings 6:17). God blinded the Syrians to the heavenly army that surrounded them, and Israel captured its enemy.

Whatever enemy you face at the crossroads of your life, remember that the faithful Lord is with you. By His Spirit, He will guide you and enable you to overcome your fear and failure.

"With God all things are possible."

MARK 10:27

You are my rock and my fortress;
Therefore, for Your name's sake,
Lead me and guide me.

PSALM 31:3

Whenever I am afraid,

I will trust in You.

In God (I will praise His word),

In God I have put my trust;

I will not fear.

PSALM 56:3–4

You are my hiding place;

You shall preserve me from trouble;

You shall surround me with songs of

deliverance.

PSALM 32:7

THE ABCs OF LOVE

Despite what this title suggests, there is nothing simple about love. The concept may be easy enough to understand: "You shall love your neighbor as yourself" (Matthew 22:39). But it's difficult to love people who have wronged us, think differently, or have conflicting values—especially when we're related to or rooming with them!

But God can enable you to love. Love for others that is rooted in God's love has staying power. In contrast to the world's brand of caring, love is resilient. It refuses to run away. It doesn't bail out when the sea gets stormy.

Christlike love has the fundamental traits of the ABCs of love. It says, "I **a**ccept you as you are. I look for the **b**est in you. And when you hurt, I **c**are." Extend this kind of love and you'll be blessed.

Love suffers long and is kind; love does not envy. . . . [Love] bears all things, believes all things, hopes all things, endures all things. Love never fails.

1 CORINTHIANS 13:4, 7–8

By this we know love, because He laid down His life for us. And we also ought to lay down our lives for the brethren. . . . My little children, let us not love in word or in tongue, but in deed and in truth.

1 JOHN 3:16, 18

Be imitators of God as dear children. And walk in love, as Christ also has loved us and given Himself for us, an offering and a sacrifice to God for a sweet-smelling aroma.

EPHESIANS 5:1–2

Neither death nor life, nor angels nor principalities nor powers, nor things present nor things to come, nor height nor depth, nor any other created thing, shall be able to separate us from the love of God which is in Christ Jesus our Lord.

ROMANS 8:38-39

For the LORD is good;
His mercy is everlasting,
And His truth endures to all generations.

PSALM 100:5

GOD'S MORNING MESSAGE

Have you ever stopped to think what an encouraging message we find in the dawn of a new day? With the sunrise, God shows His faithfulness and the grace of a fresh start. When you open your eyes to the morning sunlight, He stands willing to share the day with you and ready to provide whatever guidance, courage, and joy you will open yourself to receive from Him.

As you start the day, yield your heart and your agenda to God. Trust in His deep "I sent Jesus to the cross" love for you. He knows your circumstances, your worries, and your delights, and He hears your prayers.

Your gracious God, your heavenly Father, wants you to trust in Him with all your heart. Receive God's morning message of His love and a new day. Greet Him and then walk with Him throughout your day.

Through the LORD's mercies we are not
    consumed,
Because His compassions fail not.
They are new every morning;
Great is Your faithfulness.

LAMENTATIONS 3:22-23

You, O Lord, are a God full of compassion,
    and gracious,
Longsuffering and abundant in mercy and
    truth.

PSALM 86:15

I love the LORD, because He has heard
My voice and my supplications.
Because He has inclined His ear to me,
Therefore I will call upon Him as long as
    I live.

PSALM 116:1-2

My voice You shall hear in the morning,
    O LORD;
In the morning I will direct it to You,
And I will look up.

PSALM 5:3

FIRST PLACE

For a moment, think of your future like a blank canvas. Imagine all that could lie ahead! What will unfold depends largely on your priorities. Whom or what will you choose to place first in your life? What overriding goal or value will guide your steps and influence your decisions?

As you think about those questions, consider this wisdom from the Jewish Talmud: "Man is born with his hands clenched; he dies with his hands wide open. Entering life he desires to grasp everything; leaving the world, all that he possessed has slipped away."

What do you picture yourself reaching for? What will you choose to pursue? If you give first place to developing a relationship with Jesus Christ, your future will be bright, adventurous, and satisfying.

What things were gain to me, these I have counted loss for Christ. Yet indeed I also count all things loss for the excellence of the knowledge of Christ Jesus my Lord, for whom I have suffered the loss of all things, and count them as rubbish, that I may gain Christ.

PHILIPPIANS 3:7–8

"For what profit is it to a man if he gains the whole world, and loses his own soul?"

MATTHEW 16:26

"Do not seek what you should eat or what you should drink, nor have an anxious mind. . . . Your Father knows that you need these things. But seek the kingdom of God, and all these things shall be added to you."

LUKE 12:29–31

TIME WITH GOD

S pending time alone with God is essential to living in a way that honors and glorifies Him. You may have heard that fact as well as this one for years: we should include in our daily schedules a one-on-one appointment with the Lord.

During those minutes, read and meditate on His Word. If you're not sure where to start, websites and various ministries like BibleGateway.com, BibleHub.com, and Navigators.org offer reading plans and study tools. Also spend time praying, and be sure to include time to listen for God to respond. Know that choosing to be alone with God in His marvelous creation provides a wonderful opportunity both to praise Him and to hear from Him.

Wisdom is evident in your choice to make

quiet minutes with God a priority. May your time with God make His love for you more real and sensitize you to His guiding and strengthening presence in your life.

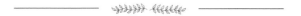

Draw near to God and He will draw near to you.

JAMES 4:8

Blessed are those who keep His testimonies, Who seek Him with the whole heart!

PSALM 119:2

You will keep him in perfect peace, Whose mind is stayed on You, Because he trusts in You.

ISAIAH 26:3

I rise before the dawning of the morning,

And cry for help;

I hope in Your word.

My eyes are awake through the night

    watches,

That I may meditate on Your word.

PSALM 119:147–148

Seek the LORD while He may be found,

Call upon Him while He is near.

ISAIAH 55:6

CULTIVATING CHARACTER

A s you begin this new chapter of your life, consider the kind of person God wants you to be.

God wants men and women who give their hearts completely to Him. God is not looking for magnificent specimens of humanity; God desires His people to have Christlike hearts. The King of kings wants, for instance, genuinely humble servants who live with integrity and find joy in serving their Lord and Savior Jesus Christ.

Today's world—and you undoubtedly know this all too well—is concerned about externals and accomplishments that others see. But that focus will only distract you and derail your efforts to be a friend of God. The Almighty is not impressed by appearances. He always focuses on the inward qualities, the character that shines His light in this dark world. Cultivating that character is worth your time and the discipline you invest in it.

"For the LORD does not see as man sees; for man looks at the outward appearance, but the LORD looks at the heart."

1 SAMUEL 16:7

Abstain from every form of evil. . . . And may your whole spirit, soul, and body be preserved blameless at the coming of our Lord Jesus Christ.

1 THESSALONIANS 5:22-23

"Let your light so shine before men, that they may see your good works and glorify your Father in heaven."

MATTHEW 5:16

Add to your faith virtue, to virtue knowledge, to knowledge self-control, to self-control perseverance, to perseverance godliness, to godliness brotherly kindness, and to brotherly kindness love. For if these things are yours and abound, you will be neither barren nor unfruitful in the knowledge of our Lord Jesus Christ.

2 PETER 1:5–8

ACCEPTANCE AND TRUST

A much-loved member of the congregation was diagnosed with cancer. From an earthly perspective, this man's prognosis was discouraging, but his faith was strong. He knew the Lord was in charge, and he was at peace with whatever plan the Lord had for his life.

The Lord is definitely in charge of the circumstances you face now and will confront in the future. Accepting this truth will help you cope with those circumstances. But God doesn't always—or even usually—tell us why a situation is what it is. With or without an explanation, we are wise to choose to accept life's challenges and commit them to the Lord.

Acceptance means taking God's hand in absolutely every situation in which we find ourselves. Acceptance is looking into our heavenly Father's face with trust and gratitude, reminding ourselves that He is indeed our Good Shepherd, guiding us, protecting us, and taking care of us. We bring Him glory when we choose to trust in those truths.

The Lord has established His throne in
    heaven,
And His kingdom rules over all.

PSALM 103:19

"I am the good shepherd; and I know My sheep, and am known by My own. As the Father knows Me, even so I know the Father; and I lay down My life for the sheep."

JOHN 10:14–15

I will call upon the Lord, who is worthy to be
praised;
So shall I be saved from my enemies.

PSALM 18:3

For You will light my lamp;
The Lord my God will enlighten my darkness.
For by You I can run against a troop,
By my God I can leap over a wall.

PSALM 18:28-29

BLACK, WHITE, AND GRAY

G ood and bad. Right and wrong. Those distinctions aren't always so clear.

These days it seems like morals come in various shades of gray. Wrong doesn't seem so wrong anymore. Right doesn't always seem wise. Honesty seems overrated— and why take responsibility for anything? Surely your situation is someone else's fault! Fairness, loyalty, courtesy, and respect are endangered character traits.

Against this gray background, you will shine brightly for the Lord as you choose to live with integrity, treat people with respect, and prove yourself a responsible person who is willing to work hard. From God's authoritative perspective, black and white exist. He will help you choose among the black, white, and gray. Then He will always be pleased, and you will never regret it.

"This is what I commanded them, saying, 'Obey My voice, and I will be your God, and you shall be My people. And walk in all the ways that I have commanded you, that it may be well with you.'"

JEREMIAH 7:23

Depart from evil and do good.

PSALM 34:14

"Whatever you want men to do to you, do also to them."

MATTHEW 7:12

A good name is to be chosen rather than
   great riches,
Loving favor rather than silver and gold.

PROVERBS 22:1

GOD'S INSTRUCTION BOOK

When we name Jesus our Savior and Lord, we are choosing to follow the instructions He set forth in His Word. If that sounds restrictive, remember that, like any good parent, God sets boundaries and establishes rules for His children's good.

How well do you know God's Instruction Book? Consider joining a Bible study. Maybe you know Scripture fairly well but fall short (we all do) when it comes to application. God will help you learn how He wants you to live, and He will help you live that way. Just ask for His help!

God's Instruction Book will, like any owner's manual, show you shortcuts, steer you away from obstacles, and help you troubleshoot. Rely on it.

We know that the Son of God has come and has given us an understanding, that we may know Him who is true; and we are in Him who is true, in His Son Jesus Christ. This is the true God and eternal life.

1 JOHN 5:20

Apply your heart to instruction,
And your ears to words of knowledge. . . .
Buy the truth, and do not sell it,
Also wisdom and instruction and
    understanding.

PROVERBS 23:12, 23

Through wisdom a house is built,
And by understanding it is established;
By knowledge the rooms are filled
With all precious and pleasant riches.

PROVERBS 24:3-4

BEARING FRUIT

I grew up in Oregon where fruit trees abound. Walking among the cherry trees and through the apple orchards, smelling the blossoms, and later in the season, eating fruit right off the trees was fun for me as a kid and a delight when I got older.

Like those orchards, a Christian's fruitful life is to be sweet, refreshing, nourishing, fragrant, sustaining, and simply delightful to be around. And like those productive cherry and apple trees, such a life does not just magically happen. Fruit trees require careful cultivation if they are to be productive. Similarly, spiritual fruit results when we develop a deeper, more consistent walk with Jesus by investing time and attention every day.

Our spiritual lives become fruitful when we open our schedules and our hearts to the work of the Holy Spirit. Communing and cooperating with Him transforms us into bearers of God's character.

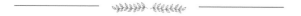

The fruit of the Spirit is love, joy, peace, longsuffering, kindness, goodness, faithfulness, gentleness, self-control. Against such there is no law.

GALATIANS 5:22–23

We . . . do not cease to pray for you, and to ask that you may be filled with the knowledge of His will in all wisdom and spiritual understanding; that you may walk worthy of the Lord, fully pleasing Him, being fruitful in every good work and increasing in the knowledge of God.

COLOSSIANS 1:9–10

His delight is in the law of the Lord,

And in His law he meditates day and night.

He shall be like a tree

Planted by the rivers of water,

That brings forth its fruit in its season.

PSALM 1:2-3

"I am the vine, you are the branches. He who abides in Me, and I in him, bears much fruit; for without Me you can do nothing. . . . By this My Father is glorified, that you bear much fruit; so you will be My disciples."

JOHN 15:5, 8

MONEY CAN'T BUY EVERYTHING

It's a dangerous and false belief, but often people consider themselves safe and secure because they have a significant amount of money. It never makes sense to trust in riches that can isolate us, distract us, and vanish without warning. It is also dangerous to pursue riches at all costs because there are many things money cannot buy.

- Money can buy medicine, but not health.
- Money can buy a house, but not a home.
- Money can buy company, but not friendship.
- Money can buy food, but not an appetite.
- Money can buy a bed, but not sleep.
- Money can buy the good life, but not eternal life.

God alone is able to provide in abundance all we need and all that money cannot buy. As the first-century Roman philosopher Seneca said—and his words are just as true today—"Money has never yet made anyone rich."

How much better to get wisdom than gold!

PROVERBS 16:16

The love of money is a root of all kinds of evil, for which some have strayed from the faith in their greediness.

1 TIMOTHY 6:10

"Take heed and beware of covetousness, for one's life does not consist in the abundance of the things he possesses."

LUKE 12:15

IT'S YOUR CHOICE!

We can feel small and powerless in this world of big government, big corporations, and big books of laws. But we do have control over a very powerful something that can have a significant impact on our lives.

We have the opportunity on a daily—perhaps even hourly—basis to choose our attitude. Our outlook may contribute more to our lives than our past, our education, or our bank account. Attitude can make the difference between success and failure, influence how circumstances in life unfold, and determine what relationships develop. The perspective we choose can cripple us or keep us moving.

When your attitude is right, there is no barrier too high, no valley too deep, no dream too big, and no challenge too great for you.

So rather than fret about things you can't change, work on changing the one thing you can—your mindset. It's your choice!

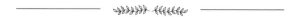

Be renewed in the spirit of your mind,
and . . . put on the new man which
was created according to God, in true
righteousness and holiness.

EPHESIANS 4:23-24

As he thinks in his heart, so is he.

PROVERBS 23:7

My soul shall be joyful in the LORD;
It shall rejoice in His salvation.

PSALM 35:9

AMAZING GRACE

The classic song "Amazing Grace" has been sung by the best professional singers on Broadway and television, by worship leaders and congregations, at weddings and funerals. It all started in the late eighteenth century, when British clergyman John Newton wrote the lyrics "Amazing grace! How sweet the sound that saved a wretch like me!" Newton used the word "wretch" to describe all of humanity: every single one of us is unworthy to be called a child of God.

Yet God graciously offers us forgiveness for our sins, and His Son made that forgiveness possible by His death and resurrection. When we confess our sins and are forgiven and cleansed by our holy and almighty God, He adopts us, calls us His children, and blesses and guides us. God's grace truly is amazing!

By grace you have been saved through faith,
and that not of yourselves; it is the gift of
God, not of works, lest anyone should boast.

EPHESIANS 2:8-9

He chose us in Him before the foundation
of the world . . . having predestined us to
adoption as sons by Jesus Christ to Himself,
according to the good pleasure of His will.

EPHESIANS 1:4-5

When the kindness and the love of God our
Savior toward man appeared, not by works
of righteousness which we have done, but
according to His mercy He saved us, through
the washing of regeneration and renewing of
the Holy Spirit, whom He poured out on us
abundantly.

TITUS 3:4-6

LIVING IN THE PRESENT

S ufficient for the day is its own trouble,"
said Jesus (Matthew 6:34). The alternatives
to focusing on today—regretting yesterday and
worrying about tomorrow—waste time and
energy. After all, you can do nothing about
either!

Living in the present, focused on the Lord
as you deal with the day's challenges, is a
spiritually, emotionally, mentally, and even
physically healthy way to live. Begin each
day by acknowledging God as Lord of your
life and asking Him to help you stay aware of
His presence. Walking with God and relying
on His guidance, strength, and wisdom will
become easier with practice.

And when you walk with God and experience His continuous guidance, strength, and
wisdom in the present day, you will be able to

handle whatever life brings. God will always supply the grace you need as the day unfolds.

Trust in the Lord with all your heart,
And lean not on your own understanding;
In all your ways acknowledge Him,
And He shall direct your paths.

PROVERBS 3:5–6

My help comes from the Lord,
Who made heaven and earth.

PSALM 121:2

God is able to make all grace abound toward you, that you, always having all sufficiency in all things, may have an abundance for every good work.

2 CORINTHIANS 9:8

TRUSTING GOD

The call to trust the Lord appears more than sixty times in the Bible, and the concept is implied in other commands, such as "Do not fear" and "Do not worry."

In Proverbs 3:5, for instance, we read, "Trust in the LORD with all your heart." In Psalm 37:3, God adds another step: "Trust in the LORD, and do good." Isaiah 26:4 says, "Trust in the LORD forever, for in YAH, the LORD, is everlasting strength."

Trusting that Jesus is God's Son who died for our sins is the pathway to a personal relationship with God; to knowing the peace, joy, contentment, and hope that relationship brings; and to life eternal with Him in heaven.

Trust keeps us aware of our need for God's presence with us. In fact, life-giving trust is walking hand in hand with Jesus every day.

Trusting the Lord is key to living a God-honoring life.

[Look] unto Jesus, the author and finisher of our faith, who for the joy that was set before Him endured the cross, despising the shame, and has sat down at the right hand of the throne of God.

HEBREWS 12:2

The blood of Jesus Christ His Son cleanses us from all sin.

1 JOHN 1:7

God has sent His only begotten Son into the world, that we might live through Him. In this is love, not that we loved God, but that He loved us and sent His Son to be the propitiation for our sins.

1 JOHN 4:9-10

By this we know love, because He laid down His life for us. And we also ought to lay down our lives for the brethren.

1 JOHN 3:16

GOD'S VERY PRESENT HELP

All around us people are working hard to be successful—whatever their definition of *success* is. For some, success is putting food on the table; for others, it's the corner office; and for most, it's something in between. Whatever their goal, these people are probably relying on their own strength.

What goals do you have? Maybe you have twenty-, ten-, and five-year goals. Whose power are you relying on to reach those goals? The Lord is available to you. Don't wait until a crisis occurs to turn to Him. He is ready and waiting to help you reach the goals that (ideally) He helped you establish. He loves you and wants to be involved in your life. He has promised to strengthen you and help you.

Walk with the Lord through each day. Let Him be your very present help.

God is our refuge and strength,

A very present help in trouble.

PSALM 46:1

"Fear not, for I am with you;

Be not dismayed, for I am your God.

I will strengthen you,

Yes, I will help you,

I will uphold you with My righteous right

hand."

ISAIAH 41:10

Be of good courage,

And He shall strengthen your heart,

All you who hope in the LORD.

PSALM 31:24

I take pleasure in infirmities, in reproaches, in needs, in persecutions, in distresses, for Christ's sake. For when I am weak, then I am strong.

2 CORINTHIANS 12:10

"When you pass through the waters, I will be
    with you;
And through the rivers, they shall not
    overflow you.
When you walk through the fire, you shall
    not be burned,
Nor shall the flame scorch you."

ISAIAH 43:2

THE VALUE OF
GOD'S WISDOM

Many verses in Proverbs invite us to acquire wisdom and understanding. God knows that we profit more from these riches than we do from much silver or fine gold (Proverbs 3:14). In Proverbs 3 we also read that wisdom is the "tree of life to those who take hold of her, and happy are all who retain her" (v. 18).

When you study God's lessons in Proverbs and learn what He teaches, you acquire wisdom. As you apply those lessons to the way you live, you will realize obeying God is the pathway to the contented life in Christ that God wants for you, His child. "Your foot will not stumble. When you lie down, you will not be afraid. . . . For the LORD will be your confidence" (Proverbs 3:23–24, 26). His wisdom is beyond price or value.

Get wisdom! Get understanding!
Do not forget, nor turn away from the words
   of my mouth.

PROVERBS 4:5

When a man's ways please the LORD,
He makes even his enemies to be at peace
   with him.

PROVERBS 16:7

Godliness with contentment is great gain.

1 TIMOTHY 6:6

UNDERSTANDING
AND OBEYING

James recognized the gap between understanding and obeying. He wrote, "Be doers of the word, and not hearers only" (James 1:22).

Students tend to become very skilled in reading and understanding the biblical text. Those very words, however, call for an active response. Our greatest struggle as believers is not trying to understand or identify God's will; instead, we struggle to *obey* His will. It's not that we find ourselves mystified and therefore paralyzed! Instead, we find ourselves stubborn, even rebellious.

We know what God wants. We read it in Scripture, we hear it taught from the pulpit, and we feel the Holy Spirit's nudge. Yet we often ignore commands that He issues for our good. We understand, yet we don't obey.

How do you really want to live?

"The Lord G<small>OD</small> has opened My ear;
And I was not rebellious,
Nor did I turn away."

ISAIAH 50:5

Samuel said:
"Has the L<small>ORD</small> as great delight in burnt
    offerings and sacrifices,
As in obeying the voice of the L<small>ORD</small>?
Behold, to obey is better than sacrifice,
And to heed than the fat of rams."

1 SAMUEL 15:22

He stores up sound wisdom for the upright;
He is a shield to those who walk uprightly.

PROVERBS 2:7

SOUNDS SIMPLE

God's wisdom is timeless, as a classic hymn from 1887 illustrates:

Trust and obey, for there's no other way
To be happy in Jesus, but to trust and obey.

That directive sounds so simple: trust and obey. We can't dispute the wisdom. We know we have no better options than God! We understand the value of obeying His commands. And we know we fall short in our trusting and obeying.

At a crossroads like a graduation, you have an opportunity to choose to trust God. Perhaps it's helpful to remember that whatever God calls you to do, He gives you the ability and strength to do it. So, by the power of His Spirit, you can choose to trust God despite how foggy or even frightening the future may be.

Trust and obey: it sounds simple, and it is.

Blessed are all those who put their trust in Him.

PSALM 2:12

It is better to trust in the LORD
Than to put confidence in man.

PSALM 118:8

The LORD will again rejoice over you for good as He rejoiced over your fathers, if you obey the voice of the LORD your God . . . and if you turn to the LORD your God with all your heart and with all your soul.

DEUTERONOMY 30:9–10

GOD'S GENEROUS GRACE

Every single person who has ever named Jesus as Savior and Lord is a sinner saved by God's grace. Like fish who don't recognize water, though, often we don't easily identify our sinfulness. God graciously reveals to us both our sin and the means of forgiveness He has made available to us. God helps us understand that He gave His only Son—the sinless sacrificial Lamb—to be crucified as payment for our sins so that you and I might be forgiven, receive the gift of salvation and eternal life, and enjoy direct access to our heavenly Father anytime, day or night.

God's generous grace saves us from the consequences of our sin and compels us to live a life of gratitude, a life that glorifies Him as we share His love and the gospel truth.

The next day John [the Baptist] saw Jesus coming toward him, and said, "Behold! The Lamb of God who takes away the sin of the world!"

JOHN 1:29

In Him we have redemption through His blood, the forgiveness of sins, according to the riches of His grace which He made to abound toward us.

EPHESIANS 1:7-8

Thanks be to God for His indescribable gift [Jesus]!

2 CORINTHIANS 9:15

For He Himself is our peace. . . . For through Him we both have access by one Spirit to the Father.

EPHESIANS 2:14, 18

NO WORRIES!

Worrying is a waste of time. Consider, for instance, how many times you have been anxious about circumstances that never materialized or a problem that was resolved sooner than expected and without your input. You realized then that you hadn't needed to worry!

God wants you to "be anxious for nothing" and to pray (Philippians 4:6). In other words, don't keep anything from the Lord. Lay before Him in prayer all your concerns—big and small and everything in between.

"No worries" is a great attitude. Give your scary circumstances to the Lord, and don't take them back again. Those concerns could not be in better hands than His.

Be merciful to me, O God, be merciful to me!
For my soul trusts in You;
And in the shadow of Your wings I will make
my refuge,
Until these calamities have passed by.

PSALM 57:1

[Cast] all your care upon Him, for He cares
for you.

1 PETER 5:7

"Behold, I am the LORD, the God of all flesh. Is
there anything too hard for Me?"

JEREMIAH 32:27

Trust in Him at all times, you people;
Pour out your heart before Him;
God is a refuge for us.

PSALM 62:8

UNLIMITED PRAYER

Think about what an amazing privilege and blessing it is to be able to pray to almighty God. He is holy, and we are not. He is divine and infinite; we are human and limited. He is kind, generous, and compassionate, and we . . . have our good moments!

Despite our less-than-shining histories, we are free to go before God anytime, about anything, and from anywhere we find ourselves. God hears our prayers around the clock. God, our heavenly Father, cares about everything we care about. And God, who is everywhere at all times, will hear us wherever we happen to be when we feel like talking or crying out for help.

We have an unlimited opportunity to pray unlimited prayers to our unlimited God! It's wise and wonderful to turn to Him whatever the time, whatever the topic.

Let us therefore come boldly to the throne of grace, that we may obtain mercy and find grace to help in time of need.

HEBREWS 4:16

The effective, fervent prayer of a righteous man avails much.

JAMES 5:16

The LORD has heard my supplication;
The LORD will receive my prayer.

PSALM 6:9

Certainly God has heard me;

He has attended to the voice of my prayer.

Blessed be God,

Who has not turned away my prayer,

Nor His mercy from me!

PSALM 66:19-20

Now this is the confidence that we have in
Him, that if we ask anything according to His
will, He hears us.

1 JOHN 5:14

NO FOOTHOLD FOR PRIDE

Christlikeness and pride cannot exist in the same heart. Look at some examples:

When someone is truly giving—generous with time, possessions, energy, and money—pride can't get a foothold in that person's heart.

When someone unselfishly puts a friend's needs ahead of his own, pride can't get a foothold in his heart.

When the young couple puts off a trip to Hawaii and instead goes on a short-term mission trip, pride doesn't get a foothold in their hearts.

When an athlete makes winning as a team more important than being acknowledged for an individual performance, pride can't get a foothold.

When you sacrificially love others with Jesus' love, you keep pride from getting a foothold in your heart.

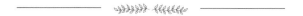

Let nothing be done through selfish ambition or conceit, but in lowliness of mind let each esteem others better than himself. Let each of you look out not only for his own interests, but also for the interests of others.

PHILIPPIANS 2:3-4

Beloved, let us love one another, for love is of God; and everyone who loves is born of God and knows God.

1 JOHN 4:7

The generous soul will be made rich,
And he who waters will also be watered
   himself.

PROVERBS 11:25

Do not forget to do good and to share, for
with such sacrifices God is well pleased.

HEBREWS 13:16

PRAYER'S BOTTOM LINE

Here is a simple fact that serves as a navigational device for all kinds of relationships: people can't read your mind. You need to ask for what you need or want!

God *can* read your mind, yet He still wants you to ask for what you need and even what you want. Jesus knew that about His Father, and He acted on that knowledge. In fact, in the garden of Gethsemane on the night He was arrested, Jesus pleaded before His Father with such intensity that He sweat blood.

Jesus did not want to die, so He prayed passionately: "Abba, Father, all things are possible for You. Take this cup away from Me; nevertheless, not what I will, but what You will" (Mark 14:36).

If we are wise, the bottom line of Jesus' prayer will always be our bottom line too: "Your will be done" (Matthew 26:42).

[Jesus] said to them, "When you pray, say:
Our Father in heaven,
Hallowed be Your name.
Your kingdom come.
Your will be done."

LUKE 11:2

Know that the LORD, He is God;
It is He who has made us, and not we
ourselves;
We are His people and the sheep of His
pasture.

PSALM 100:3

Is anyone among you suffering? Let him
pray.

JAMES 5:13

Teach me to do Your will,
For You are my God;
Your Spirit is good.
Lead me in the land of uprightness.

PSALM 143:10

PEOPLE NOTICE!

Life calls for intentionality. Why are you doing what you do? Are you being deliberate about using your time and energy? Don't let life just sort of happen. Instead:

- Establish a firm foundation for your plans and goals: be biblical.
- Live with integrity according to the truths of Scripture: be authentic.
- Choose compassion: be gracious.
- Stay current: be relevant.

When we live this way, we incarnate our faith in Jesus, and people notice. Perhaps God will use our purposefulness, kindness, concern, or wisdom to prompt others to wonder what makes us different. When they question you, "be ready to give a defense to everyone who asks you a reason for the hope that is in you" (1 Peter 3:15). People in the first century noticed Jesus-followers, and people in the twenty-first century will too!

He who walks with integrity walks securely,
But he who perverts his ways will become
    known.

PROVERBS 10:9

Be of one mind, having compassion for one another; love as brothers, be tenderhearted, be courteous; not returning evil for evil or reviling for reviling, but on the contrary blessing.

1 PETER 3:8-9

But in all things we commend ourselves as ministers of God . . . by purity, by knowledge, by longsuffering, by kindness, by the Holy Spirit, by sincere love.

2 CORINTHIANS 6:4, 6

"By this all will know that you are My disciples, if you have love for one another."

JOHN 13:35

GOD'S WILL

The Ten Commandments offer insight into God's will for our lives: they reveal the fact that He is more concerned about our relationship with Him and our character than He is about which job we take or even whom we marry. That's not to say He doesn't provide guidelines for those decisions. Through His Spirit, His Word, and His people, He will "direct your paths" (Proverbs 3:6).

Doing the will of God, however, can be difficult. After all, we each have our own will, and we want what we want! We need to remind ourselves that our heavenly Father knows what is good for us. When we surrender our will to His, we can trust His Spirit to guide us in the best direction.

I beseech you therefore, brethren, by the mercies of God, that you present your bodies a living sacrifice, holy, acceptable to God, which is your reasonable service. . . . Be transformed by the renewing of your mind, that you may prove what is that good and acceptable and perfect will of God.

ROMANS 12:1–2

I will instruct you and teach you in the way
    you should go;
I will guide you with My eye.

PSALM 32:8

He has shown you, O man, what is good;

And what does the Lord require of you

But to do justly,

To love mercy,

And to walk humbly with your God?

MICAH 6:8

We have had human fathers who corrected us, and we paid them respect. Shall we not much more readily be in subjection to the Father of spirits and live?

HEBREWS 12:9

BE DIFFERENT

In the twenty-first century, we see many different worldviews and lifestyles. Television, print media, and social media show us people pursuing worldly ambitions, defining their own morality, and answering to no one on earth or in heaven. Our world is not always friendly to Christians or Christian values.

By God's gracious provision, we have His Holy Spirit to guide our decisions, however countercultural they may be. Only a radically different mindset and resolve strengthened by the Holy Spirit can enable us to stand alone—and stand for God—in a society with opposing values and goals.

Identify your values, and uphold them with the strength of the Spirit. Dare to be different!

Keep sound wisdom and discretion;
So they will be life to your soul
And grace to your neck.
Then you will walk safely in your way,
And your foot will not stumble.

PROVERBS 3:21-23

"When they bring you to the synagogues
and magistrates and authorities, do not
worry about how or what you should answer,
or what you should say. For the Holy Spirit
will teach you in that very hour what you
ought to say."

LUKE 12:11-12

The Lord stood with me and strengthened
me, so that the message might be preached
fully through me.

2 TIMOTHY 4:17

FREEDOM IN CHRIST

The freedom we have in Christ is a wonderful blessing! In light of that fact, Paul called believers to hang on to the "liberty by which Christ has made us free"; he also warned Christ-followers not to get tangled again with "a yoke of bondage" to the Law (Galatians 5:1). In theory, perfectly adhering to God's law would lead to our salvation, but such obedience is humanly impossible.

Though in our time we aren't tempted to sacrifice animals in obedience to Old Testament laws, we may be tempted to live according to the world's standards. To counter the very human tendency to conform to the world, Paul urged us "not [to] use liberty as an opportunity for the flesh, but through love serve one another" (Galatians 5:13).

Free in Christ, may we choose to love.

There is therefore now no condemnation to those who are in Christ Jesus, who do not walk according to the flesh, but according to the Spirit. For the law of the Spirit of life in Christ Jesus has made me free from the law of sin and death.

ROMANS 8:1-2

Having been set free from sin, and having become slaves of God, you have your fruit to holiness, and the end, everlasting life.

ROMANS 6:22

"Whoever desires to become great among you shall be your servant. And whoever of you desires to be first shall be slave of all. For even the Son of Man did not come to be served, but to serve, and to give His life a ransom for many."

MARK 10:43-45

YOUR PROMISE-KEEPING GOD

God's Word contains thousands of promises God has made to His people. Whether there are three thousand or seven thousand promises (both numbers have been reported) is not as important as the fact that God will keep every single one of them!

Whatever challenges you must address, whatever decisions you face, and whatever hurts are weighing you down, God promises to give you strength, guidance, and comfort. In other words, God is with you, "for He Himself has said, 'I will never leave you nor forsake you'" (Hebrews 13:5).

We can take this promise to the bank of life and rest in the truth of God's presence with us. The Lord will indeed be with you wherever you go and whatever you do—He is *El Shaddai*, the All-Sufficient One. That's a promise!

God is not a man, that He should lie,

Nor a son of man, that He should repent.

Has He said, and will He not do?

Or has He spoken, and will He not make it
good?

NUMBERS 23:19

[The Lord] will fulfill the desire of those who
fear Him;

He also will hear their cry and save them.

The Lord preserves all who love Him.

PSALM 145:19–20

I love the Lord, because He has heard

My voice and my supplications.

Because He has inclined His ear to me,

Therefore I will call upon Him as long as
I live.

PSALM 116:1–2

COUNT YOUR BLESSINGS

Count your blessings, name them one by one,
Count your blessings, see what God hath
*   done!*

Ordained Methodist Episcopal preacher Johnson Oatman Jr. wrote the words of this hymn in the late nineteenth century, and the encouragement he offered is as wise and relevant today as it was then.

The refrain of this great hymn calls us to approach God with a grateful heart and to thank Him for the many blessings we receive from Him each day. Gratitude not only lightens our step, it keeps our eyes on the Lord, the Giver of all good gifts (James 1:17).

In addition, it's amazing how God works in our lives when we open our hearts to His

love. And we do exactly that when we count
our many blessings and thank God for them.

Bless the Lord, O my soul,
And forget not all His benefits.

PSALM 103:2

It is good to give thanks to the Lord,
And to sing praises to Your name, O Most
    High;
To declare Your lovingkindness in the
    morning,
And Your faithfulness every night.

PSALM 92:1-2

Enter into His gates with thanksgiving,

And into His courts with praise.

Be thankful to Him, and bless His name.

For the Lord is good;

His mercy is everlasting,

And His truth endures to all generations.

PSALM 100:4-5

Through the Lord's mercies we are not

    consumed,

Because His compassions fail not.

They are new every morning;

Great is Your faithfulness.

LAMENTATIONS 3:22-23

THE POWER OF FORGIVENESS

J esus was very direct: *Treat people the way you want them to treat you* (see Matthew 7:12). And Jesus was very specific: "Forgive, and you will be forgiven" (Luke 6:37). We treat others the way we want to be treated by asking forgiveness when we fail and extending forgiveness when they fail.

The power of forgiveness is amazing! Forgiveness empties the ammunition in the hurt party's weapon of revenge. Forgiveness of another Jesus-follower brings healing and peace to both hearts.

We are more able to extend forgiveness when we take one simple but not necessarily easy step: we choose humility and recognize that our own sin sent Jesus to the cross to die.

When we who have been forgiven extend forgiveness, we set free the people we hurt as well as ourselves. Don't wait any longer. Look at the cross, and then just do it—unleash the power of forgiveness.

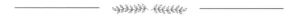

God demonstrates His own love toward us, in that while we were still sinners, Christ died for us.

ROMANS 5:8

"If your brother sins against you, rebuke him; and if he repents, forgive him. And if he sins against you seven times in a day, and seven times in a day returns to you, saying, 'I repent,' you shall forgive him."

LUKE 17:3-4

"If you forgive men their trespasses, your heavenly Father will also forgive you."

MATTHEW 6:14

Put on tender mercies . . . bearing with one another, and forgiving one another, if anyone has a complaint against another; even as Christ forgave you, so you also must do.

COLOSSIANS 3:12–13

LEAVE THE PAST
IN THE PAST

Some of the unhappiest people around are those who focus on the past and feel haunted by *If only . . . Why did* [or *didn't*] *I . . . ? What was I thinking?*

That kind of thinking is, simply put, a waste of time. You can change nothing that happened in the past, no matter how often you berate yourself for your mistakes and sins. God offers forgiveness and freedom from shame.

Forgetting your yesterdays means having more energy as well as more joy for today. Few joy-stealers are more effective than memories that taunt our minds. Leave the past behind and be open to the possibilities God has planned for you. His plans for you are good. In fact, they just may be far greater than anything you can imagine!

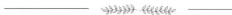

[He] is able to do exceedingly abundantly
above all that we ask or think.

EPHESIANS 3:20

If anyone is in Christ, he is a new creation;
old things have passed away; behold, all
things have become new.

2 CORINTHIANS 5:17

One thing I do, forgetting those things which
are behind and reaching forward to those things
which are ahead, I press toward the goal for the
prize of the upward call of God in Christ Jesus.

PHILIPPIANS 3:13–14

Eye has not seen, nor ear heard,
Nor have entered into the heart of man
The things which God has prepared for
    those who love Him.

1 CORINTHIANS 2:9

HOLY HUMILITY

A humble spirit is a rare commodity in the twenty-first century.

We live in a world of pride and self-righteousness, of "It's all about me," of reaching our goals no matter the toll it takes on other people. People feed our egos with statements about how great we are and how much we have accomplished. Developing a bloated self-image stands in sharp contrast to Jesus, who came down from heaven to serve us sinners by dying for us.

We can make no better response to Jesus' sacrificial death than humility. When we humble ourselves before the Lord and yield ourselves to His Spirit, we will know purpose, peace, fulfillment, and contentment. We will know the blessing and the joy of His presence with us.

When we go to the Lord in holy humility, with a heart of worship and praise, He is honored, and we are blessed.

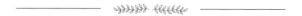

Let this mind be in you which was also in Christ Jesus, who . . . made Himself of no reputation, taking the form of a bondservant, and coming in the likeness of men.

PHILIPPIANS 2:5–7

When pride comes, then comes shame;
But with the humble is wisdom.

PROVERBS 11:2

All of you be submissive to one another, and be clothed with humility, for

"God resists the proud,
But gives grace to the humble."

1 PETER 5:5

CHOOSE FAITH

Change is part of life, and change brings stress. Graduation means change. Do you welcome it, or are you reluctant, nervous, or even fearful? Thankfully, as unknown as the future may be to you, God's got this! You don't know the future, but you can get to know Him better and therefore know peace.

Consider that God is wise, trustworthy, and good. He is powerful. He loves you, and He is near you always. He provides comfort, compassion, and hope. The better you know your God, the more easily you will welcome the future.

Right now your future is a blank canvas. Trust it—trust your very life—to the Master Artist. Choose to live by faith each day for the Lord's glory, and, as His plans for you unfold, be amazed by the beauty He creates in your life.

The word of the Lord is right,

And all His work is done in truth.

He loves righteousness and justice;

The earth is full of the goodness of the Lord.

PSALM 33:4-5

Oh, taste and see that the Lord is good;

Blessed is the man who trusts in Him!

PSALM 34:8

You, Lord, are good, and ready to forgive,

And abundant in mercy to all those who call

upon You.

PSALM 86:5

Oh, give thanks to the Lord, for He is good!

For His mercy endures forever.

PSALM 106:1

WALKING WITH GOD

If you haven't already noticed, you will soon: life is difficult. Walking with God is a day-by-day experience we are wise to choose. Why refuse guidance and companionship, especially when our Creator, the sovereign God, the Lover of our souls, is the One offering that support?

Jesus did not deny that life in this fallen world would be hard. He Himself experienced this when He walked this earth. So welcome the company of this "Man of sorrows and acquainted with grief" (Isaiah 53:3), the company of the Redeemer who brings beauty out of ashes (61:3).

As we walk with God through struggles and difficulties, He uses those fires to refine our faith and make us more like Christ. You truly can walk *with* Him throughout your life in perfect trust. God will never fail you.

Cause me to hear Your lovingkindness
    in the morning,
For in You do I trust;
Cause me to know the way in which I
    should walk,
For I lift up my soul to You.

PSALM 143:8

Though I walk in the midst of trouble,
    You will revive me.

PSALM 138:7

Teach me Your way, O Lord;
I will walk in Your truth;
Unite my heart to fear Your name.

PSALM 86:11

Blessed is every one who fears the Lord,
Who walks in His ways.

PSALM 128:1

WORSHIPPING OUR HOLY GOD

*H*oly means *set apart*. God is holy: in His divinity, He is set apart from us in our humanity.

Holy also means *free of sin*. God is holy: He is utterly free of sin; He is pure in thought, word, and deed. And we human beings are not.

And *holy* means *worthy of worship*. Our set-apart and sin-free God truly is worthy of our worship and devotion.

This glorious God loves sinful, self-centered people with an everlasting love. He gave His Son to die for us sinners; He didn't wait for us to shape up or meet certain standards. If we acknowledge our need for forgiveness and recognize Jesus as the Savior who meets that need, our holy God accepts us. So may we wholeheartedly "give unto the Lord the glory due to His name; worship the Lord in the beauty of holiness" (Psalm 29:2).

Oh come, let us worship and bow down;
Let us kneel before the Lord our Maker.
For He is our God,
And we are the people of His pasture,
And the sheep of His hand.

PSALM 95:6-7

Exalt the Lord our God,
And worship at His footstool—
He is holy.

PSALM 99:5

As He who called you is holy, you also be holy in all your conduct.

1 PETER 1:15

"For God so loved the world that He gave His only begotten Son, that whoever believes in Him should not perish but have everlasting life."

JOHN 3:16

The four living creatures, each having six wings, were full of eyes around and within. And they do not rest day or night, saying:

"Holy, holy, holy,
Lord God Almighty,
Who was and is and is to come!"

REVELATION 4:8

TEACH US CONTENTMENT

It's an advertiser's job to make us discontent, to persuade us that whatever we own is out of style, to be sure we feel dissatisfied with what we have, and to convince us that the key to our contentment is . . . whatever he or she is selling.

On our own we can do a good job fueling the fire of our discontent. We look around at all others have—but we don't see their credit card debt. We see people in prestigious jobs—but we don't know what that accomplishment has cost them. We see families who look problem-free—but we are deceiving ourselves with the thought that anyone could live in this fallen world without experiencing pain and loss.

Contentment comes when we lean on the Lord, choose to live according to His priorities, and trust Him to teach us contentment.

I have learned in whatever state I am, to be content: I know how to be abased, and I know how to abound. Everywhere and in all things I have learned both to be full and to be hungry, both to abound and to suffer need.

PHILIPPIANS 4:11–12

Let your conduct be without covetousness; be content with such things as you have.

HEBREWS 13:5

The fear of the L‍ord leads to life,
And he who has it will abide in satisfaction.

PROVERBS 19:23

"Do not lay up for yourselves treasures on
earth, where moth and rust destroy and
where thieves break in and steal; but lay up
for yourselves treasures in heaven, where
neither moth nor rust destroys and
where thieves do not break in and steal.
For where your treasure is, there your heart
will be also."

MATTHEW 6:19–21

ALL TOO RARE

There's spin, there's the hairsplitting of definitions. And there are flat-out lies told with no twinge of conscience and fabricated stories very elaborate in detail. And all of these are traps waiting to trip up their creators.

If we walk through life with integrity, though, we will not stumble because of our own words. When we choose to be honest in our speech, honest in our relationships (both personal and professional), and honest with God about our sin, we will reflect His light. We will take a stand for the light of truth in a world darkened by too many lies.

We will also know God's pleasure in us as we live with integrity. We honor Him and our fellow human beings with honesty and truth, two things that are all too rare.

He who walks with integrity walks securely.

PROVERBS 10:9

Better is the poor who walks in his integrity
Than one perverse in his ways, though he be
   rich.

PROVERBS 28:6

Let integrity and uprightness preserve me,
For I wait for You.

PSALM 25:21

Know that the Lord has set apart for Himself
   him who is godly;
The Lord will hear when I call to Him.

PSALM 4:3

AN ONGOING CONVERSATION

Vital in the life of a Christian is maintaining an ongoing conversation with God.

For starters, having daily in-depth conversations with your heavenly Father opens your heart and mind to God's wisdom. He longs to give you the knowledge you need to make good decisions.

In addition to seeking wisdom, lay before God your needs, other people's struggles, and your desires. Spend time praising God, which honors Him and fills your heart with hope and peace. Confess your sin to Him, which brings the freedom and the fresh start that come with His forgiveness. Thank Him for His many blessings, which remind you of His loving and generous presence in your life.

One more thing: check in with God throughout the day. Short prayers of thanks or quick requests for wisdom keep you in ongoing conversation with God and growing in your relationship with Him.

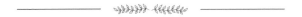

"When you pray, go into your room, and when you have shut your door, pray to your Father who is in the secret place; and your Father who sees in secret will reward you openly."

MATTHEW 6:6

I called on the LORD in distress;
The LORD answered me and set me in a
broad place.

PSALM 118:5

"Because he has set his love upon Me,
    therefore I will deliver him;
I will set him on high, because he has known
    My name.
He shall call upon Me, and I will answer him;
I will be with him in trouble;
I will deliver him and honor him.
With long life I will satisfy him,
And show him My salvation."

PSALM 91:14–16

Pray without ceasing.

1 THESSALONIANS 5:17

MAKING A DIFFERENCE

When you look in the mirror, do you see someone who loves God, someone God is using to make a difference in this lonely world?

The world offers us many pursuits, a variety of distractions, and a lot of stuff to acquire, but it offers nothing that lasts and nothing that satisfies the deep-seated human hunger for significance. A follower of Jesus chooses what satisfies today, tomorrow, and forever—and that is a relationship with Jesus.

When we walk with Jesus, His Spirit shines through us, guides our words and deeds, and enables us to love even the hard-to-love in our world. That's why we Christians remind one another that we may be the only Bible that some people ever read. What message do you want people to read when they look at your life? What difference do you want to make?

"By this all will know that you are My disciples, if you have love for one another."

JOHN 13:35

"Love your enemies, do good, and lend, hoping for nothing in return; and your reward will be great, and you will be sons of the Most High. For He is kind to the unthankful and evil. Therefore be merciful, just as your Father also is merciful."

LUKE 6:35-36

Do not be overcome by evil, but overcome evil with good.

ROMANS 12:21

Walk in wisdom toward those who are outside, redeeming the time. Let your speech always be with grace, seasoned with salt, that you may know how you ought to answer each one.

COLOSSIANS 4:5-6

"Therefore, whatever you want men to do to you, do also to them, for this is the Law and the Prophets."

MATTHEW 7:12

DON'T GO IT ALONE!

O ur heavenly Father, whose commands and instructions are full of benefits, calls us to be in community with fellow believers. (That makes extra-good sense when, as a graduate, you are stepping out into the unknown!)

Ideally, with community comes accountability. Choosing to be accountable about your walk with the Lord, though, means taking the risk of being honest and open with another believer.

Vulnerability—opening the door to your genuine self and innermost thoughts—is only one quality of people who are accountable to others for their walk with the Lord. Both parties must be able to admit the truth about how they're doing, no matter how difficult it may be. Both parties must also be teachable, willing to learn God's way, and open to biblical correction and counsel.

Don't go it alone! We believers need each other to live in a way that honors God.

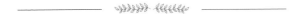

Two are better than one,
Because they have a good reward for
    their labor.
For if they fall, one will lift up his companion.
But woe to him who is alone when he falls,
For he has no one to help him up.

ECCLESIASTES 4:9–10

He who disdains instruction despises his
    own soul,
But he who heeds rebuke gets understanding.

PROVERBS 15:32

Let us consider one another in order to stir up love and good works, not forsaking the assembling of ourselves together . . . but exhorting one another.

HEBREWS 10:24–25

"For where two or three are gathered together in My name, I am there in the midst of them."

MATTHEW 18:20

FIRST THINGS FIRST

When we choose to focus on God whole-heartedly, we may see the various aspects of our lives falling into place in a new way. We may, for instance, find ourselves with time to go to church and money to put in the offering plate. We may start to consider possible jobs from the perspective of *Is this where God is calling me*? rather than *How much money will I make*?

When we trust the Lord with all our being, we allow God to be the focal point of our thoughts and our Guide for life. Our circumstances, other people, responsibilities, and even self-interest can distract us and keep us from focusing on God. But hear Jesus' promise: "Seek first the kingdom of God and His righteousness, and all these things"—food, tuition, clothing, living space, job, friends—"shall be added to you" (Matthew 6:33). Keep God first!

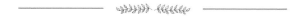

"'You shall love the LORD your God with all your heart, with all your soul, with all your mind, and with all your strength.'"

MARK 12:30

A man's heart plans his way,
But the LORD directs his steps.

PROVERBS 16:9

My eyes are ever toward the LORD,
For He shall pluck my feet out of the net.

PSALM 25:15

Those who seek the LORD shall not lack any
good thing.

PSALM 34:10

BLESSED BY JOY

What steals your joy? Is it worries about the future? A lack of job opportunities? Concern about where to live? A rocky relationship? Health issues? Newspaper headlines? The list of what can prompt worry, fear, stress, and doubt—of all that steals our joy—goes on and on.

But the Lord wants us to know joy *in Him*. As David put it, "In Your presence is fullness of joy" (Psalm 16:11). What an argument for beginning every morning alone with God, sharing our thoughts for the day and allowing His Spirit to fill us with His presence! When we release our cares and fears to our all-wise, all-loving, all-powerful God, He will give us the joy that only He can give.

Circumstances of life can make us happy, but the Lord blesses us with genuine joy.

My soul shall be joyful in the LORD;
It shall rejoice in His salvation.

PSALM 35:9

I will greatly rejoice in the LORD,
My soul shall be joyful in my God;
For He has clothed me with the garments
   of salvation,
He has covered me with the robe of
   righteousness.

ISAIAH 61:10

Your word was to me the joy and rejoicing
   of my heart;
For I am called by Your name,
O LORD God of hosts.

JEREMIAH 15:16

Let them shout for joy and be glad,

Who favor my righteous cause;

And let them say continually,

"Let the Lᴏʀᴅ be magnified,

Who has pleasure in the prosperity

   of His servant."

PSALM 35:27

For His anger is but for a moment,

His favor is for life;

Weeping may endure for a night,

But joy comes in the morning.

PSALM 30:5

OPEN THE DOOR

Jesus spoke the unpopular truth: "In the world you will have tribulation; but be of good cheer, I have overcome the world" (John 16:33). Yes, you will experience difficulties and hard times as you journey through life, but they are not the whole story. Jesus' ultimate victory over sin and death is the glorious finale! Jesus sealed that victory with His resurrection from the dead, yet skirmishes between His people and the devil continue.

So will today bring a battle? Each new day is like a package delivered to your front door. A package may be labeled "Watch out," occasionally "Danger," and even "Impossible," and those labels provoke anxiety and doubt. But notice the other labels, those written by Jesus' hand: "Hope," "Victory," "Possible," "Redeemable," and "Walk with Me." When the package of each new day arrives, open the door to Jesus.

We also glory in tribulations, knowing that tribulation produces perseverance; and perseverance, character; and character, hope. Now hope does not disappoint, because the love of God has been poured out in our hearts by the Holy Spirit who was given to us.

ROMANS 5:3-5

May the God of all grace, who called us to His eternal glory by Christ Jesus, after you have suffered a while, perfect, establish, strengthen, and settle you.

1 PETER 5:10

You have been grieved by various trials,
that the genuineness of your faith, being
much more precious than gold that perishes,
though it is tested by fire, may be found to
praise, honor, and glory at the revelation of
Jesus Christ.

1 PETER 1:6-7

"When you pass through the waters, I will be
    with you;
And through the rivers, they shall not
    overflow you.
When you walk through the fire, you shall
    not be burned,
Nor shall the flame scorch you."

ISAIAH 43:2

WHO'S IN CHARGE?

Do you know what *sovereign* means? I'm guessing you do: all-powerful, in charge, the ultimate ruler.

And God—your all-good, all-wise, all-powerful, all-loving God—is sovereign over the history of the world and over the story of your life. Is that truth impacting how you live?

We too often live as if the world revolves around us. We make decisions on our own and according to our self-interest. We are not always the servants God calls His people to be. We are not always God's light of grace and love. Bottom line, sometimes we don't live as though God is our sovereign Lord.

Your heavenly Father wants the best for you, and you can rest in the truth that His plan for you is all-good, all-wise, and all-loving. Are you living for the One who created you, the One who is truly in charge?

The Lord reigns;
Let the earth rejoice.

PSALM 97:1

The eye of the Lord is on those who fear Him,
On those who hope in His mercy. . . .
Our soul waits for the Lord;
He is our help and our shield.

PSALM 33:18, 20

Through the tender mercy of our God,
With which the Dayspring from on high has
    visited us;
To give light to those who sit in darkness
    and the shadow of death,
To guide our feet into the way of peace.

LUKE 1:78-79

THE WORDS YOU SPEAK

How many times have you said something harsh, and then wondered, *Where did that come from?* It truly is hard to control the words we say, to think before we speak. No wonder James called the tongue "an unruly evil, full of deadly poison" (3:8).

When we are living for Christ, we need to be sure that our words are honest and that we speak with kindness and grace. Nothing may be more destructive to our testimony than speaking words that are unkind or untrue.

May David's prayer be ours each day: "Let the words of my mouth and the meditation of my heart be acceptable in Your sight, O LORD, my strength and my Redeemer" (Psalm 19:14). Make sure the words you speak are the words He delights to hear.

He who would love life
And see good days,
Let him refrain his tongue from evil,
And his lips from speaking deceit.

1 PETER 3:10

Though I speak with the tongues of men and
of angels, but have not love, I have become
sounding brass or a clanging cymbal.

1 CORINTHIANS 13:1

If anyone among you thinks he is religious,
and does not bridle his tongue but deceives
his own heart, this one's religion is useless.

JAMES 1:26

Be an example to the believers in word, in
conduct, in love, in spirit, in faith, in purity.

1 TIMOTHY 4:12

HOW TO RUN WELL

Imagine living in such a way that, in the end, you hear the Lord Himself say, "Well done, good and faithful servant" (Matthew 25:21). Could there be any greater reward?

Yet living for the Lord is not easy. Thankfully, when we blow it—and all of us sin multiple times a day—we can confess our sins, receive God's forgiveness, and start fresh. Still, living a life committed to following Jesus is more like running a marathon than a forty-meter dash.

What can help you run well? Keep your eyes on Jesus who stands at the finish line. Feed your soul with the Word of God. Pray each step of the way. Run with a partner. Drink the living water of the Spirit within you.

Living for Jesus is a marathon worth running.

Let us run with endurance the race that is set before us, looking unto Jesus, the author and finisher of our faith.

HEBREWS 12:1-2

Those who wait on the Lord
Shall renew their strength;
They shall mount up with wings like eagles,
They shall run and not be weary,
They shall walk and not faint.

ISAIAH 40:31

Do you not know that those who run in a race all run, but one receives the prize? Run in such a way that you may obtain it.

1 CORINTHIANS 9:24

PICTURES OF HUMILITY

What comes to mind when you hear the word *humility*? The people of our culture might think of a doormat. Ideally, a follower of Jesus would picture a powerful steed, ready for war, but with its strength reined in and under control.

Jesus Himself modeled humility. When He chose to be human, He reined in His divine power. When He chose to wash His disciples' feet, this Rabbi took on the menial job Himself. And, in the ultimate display of strength in control, Jesus allowed Himself to be nailed to the cross, an instrument of death for murderers, rebels, and traitors.

Today humility takes the form of treating others as you want to be treated, loving your enemies, and turning the other cheek. In making those choices, you rein in the power of the ego: you die to what you want in order to live as Jesus did—as a picture of humility.

"If I then, your Lord and Teacher, have washed your feet, you also ought to wash one another's feet. For I have given you an example, that you should do as I have done to you."

JOHN 13:14-15

Being found in appearance as a man, He humbled Himself and became obedient to the point of death, even the death of the cross.

PHILIPPIANS 2:8

"I am among you as the One who serves."

LUKE 22:27

STUDY WORDS OF WISDOM

So spoke the wise father to his son, "Get wisdom!" (Proverbs 4:5). That is solid counsel for all of us. God is the ultimate Source of eternal wisdom, but not everyone turns to Him. After all, we ask for something only if we know we need it; we look for something only if we want it.

Humbly recognizing our need for wisdom does not come easily to us human beings—we love our independence. We can be very comfortable with what we already understand and what the world offers.

But when we realize we need divine wisdom, we can ask God in prayer. We can also study His Word in quest of His guidance and truth. God doesn't deliver wisdom to our door like the morning paper, but with the gift of His Spirit, Jesus has definitely made it easy for us to learn from Scripture: "The Helper, the Holy Spirit . . . will teach you all things" (John 14:26). Take time to study wise words; you'll never regret it.

All Scripture is given by inspiration of God, and is profitable for doctrine, for reproof, for correction, for instruction in righteousness, that the man of God may be complete, thoroughly equipped for every good work.

2 TIMOTHY 3:16–17

Show me Your ways, O LORD;
Teach me Your paths.
Lead me in Your truth and teach me,
For You are the God of my salvation.

PSALM 25:4–5

The mouth of the righteous speaks wisdom,

And his tongue talks of justice.

The law of his God is in his heart;

None of his steps shall slide.

PSALM 37:30-31

Happy is the man who finds wisdom,

And the man who gains understanding;

For her proceeds are better than the profits
    of silver,

And her gain than fine gold.

PROVERBS 3:13-14

THE FRUIT OF PATIENCE

In His written Word, God speaks to us through the psalmist, calling us to "rest in the LORD, and wait patiently for Him" (Psalm 37:7). The concepts of resting, waiting, and being patient are countercultural in our world of hurry-up living, where communication is instantaneous and lack of sleep is something of a status symbol.

For our own health and well-being, spiritual as well as physical, we need to rest. We need to wait for God to work. Specifically, when we face a major decision and ask God for wisdom, we need to wait patiently for Him to provide. When we are impatient, we can too easily make hasty decisions that result in problems we might have avoided.

May you yield to the work of the Spirit, so

that He may grow in your heart the fruits of His presence. One of those fruits is patience.

Imitate those who through faith and patience inherit the promises.

HEBREWS 6:12

Pursue righteousness, godliness, faith, love, patience, gentleness.

1 TIMOTHY 6:11

Whatever things were written before were written for our learning, that we through the patience and comfort of the Scriptures might have hope. Now may the God of patience and comfort grant you to be like-minded toward one another, according to Christ Jesus.

ROMANS 15:4-5

WHEN YOU WANT
TO GIVE UP

You don't see any way out; you see no hope on the horizon; you simply want to give up. Don't! Try these ideas instead.

First, know that your enemy, the devil and master deceiver, is behind your despair. Praying aloud, send him away in the name and power of Jesus.

Second, know the truth that everything—absolutely everything—is possible for almighty God.

Third, pray. Pray about what you cannot change or control. Pray about whoever frightens or agitates you, about whatever keeps you awake or breaks your heart. Move all those things from your worry list to your prayer list. When you lay at God's feet everything that is weighing you down, you will experience God's peace, an antidote to despair.

Finally, when you want to give up—when you struggle to pray and have faith—find people who will pray and believe along with you. Don't give up!

"[Satan] was a murderer from the beginning, and does not stand in the truth, because there is no truth in him. When he speaks a lie, he speaks from his own resources, for he is a liar and the father of it."

JOHN 8:44

"The things which are impossible with men are possible with God."

LUKE 18:27

If two lie down together, they will
    keep warm;
But how can one be warm alone?
Though one may be overpowered by
    another, two can withstand him.
And a threefold cord is not quickly broken.

ECCLESIASTES 4:11–12

[Be] patient in tribulation, continuing stead-
fastly in prayer.

ROMANS 12:12

LOW ON CONFIDENCE?

When Jesus is our focus, our reason for existence, we can know a confidence that pushes aside our fears and insecurities. When we focus on Jesus, we remind ourselves of His sovereignty, His faithfulness, His goodness, and His presence with us always. Keeping our eyes on our Savior and Lord can erase the joy-stealers in life. How?

- Jesus helps us look beyond our circumstances, and this long-term perspective gives us hope.
- Jesus delivers us from preoccupation with people who seem to have easier lives, nicer houses, better cars—and our satisfaction level rises.
- Looking at Jesus calms our fears about the future.

Our focus on Jesus inevitably reminds us of His love for us. If you are low on confidence, remember that His love, which took Him to the cross, can mean daily hope, courage for the future, and contentment in the present.

"When you pass through the waters, I will be
    with you;
And through the rivers, they shall not
    overflow you.
When you walk through the fire, you shall
    not be burned,
Nor shall the flame scorch you.
For I am the Lord your God,
The Holy One of Israel, your Savior."

ISAIAH 43:2-3

"Whoever comes to Me, and hears My sayings and does them, I will show you whom he is like: He is like a man building a house, who dug deep and laid the foundation on the rock. And when the flood arose, the stream beat vehemently against that house, and could not shake it, for it was founded on the rock."

LUKE 6:47-48

Do not be afraid of sudden terror,
Nor of trouble from the wicked when it
     comes;
For the LORD will be your confidence,
And will keep your foot from being caught.

PROVERBS 3:25-26

WHEN IT'S YOUR TURN

No matter how much we pray, how regularly we go to church, or how many minutes we spend reading God's Word, life in this fallen world will not be easy. It's inevitable: disappointment will come, often suddenly and unexpectedly.

When it's your turn to be disappointed, receive the disheartening situation with faith; ask God how to respond. Know that God is not surprised or overwhelmed. What has happened has challenged you, but your sovereign God is in control. Rest in His presence and receive the peace He offers.

Everyone gets to experience disappointment; take your turn with grace.

I consider that the sufferings of this present
time are not worthy to be compared with
the glory which shall be revealed in us.

ROMANS 8:18

The LORD is near to those who have a
    broken heart,
And saves such as have a contrite spirit.
Many are the afflictions of the righteous,
But the LORD delivers him out of them all.

PSALM 34:18-19

You have been a shelter for me,
A strong tower from the enemy. . . .
I will trust in the shelter of Your wings.

PSALM 61:3-4

GLORY, GRACE, TRUTH

John was an eyewitness to the God-Man who saved our souls: "We beheld His glory, the glory as of the only begotten of the Father, full of grace and truth" (John 1:14). The glory of Jesus was the divine nature of this carpenter from Nazareth. John, the rest of the disciples, and many people in Jesus' day saw the glory of God in Jesus as He revealed the Father's grace and truth.

In a world where we try to earn acceptance, respect, and even love, God blesses us with unmerited favor. In this world of darkness and hypocrisy, Jesus spoke and lived truth. He even said, "I am the way, the truth, and the life" (John 14:6).

Have you recognized Jesus as the God-Man who died for your sins? Have you acknowledged Him as your Lord as well as your Savior?

"I am the good shepherd. The good shepherd gives His life for the sheep."

JOHN 10:11

We have seen and testify that the Father has sent the Son as Savior of the world. Whoever confesses that Jesus is the Son of God, God abides in him, and he in God.

1 JOHN 4:14–15

"I am the bread of life. He who comes to Me shall never hunger, and he who believes in Me shall never thirst. . . . And this is the will of Him who sent Me, that everyone who sees the Son and believes in Him may have everlasting life; and I will raise him up at the last day."

JOHN 6:35, 40

FEARING GOD

What does it mean to fear God? Among other things, it means honoring Him as King of kings, Lord of lords, the Almighty, the Creator, the Author of history, the Righteous Judge, and the Holy One. A healthy fear of God keeps us mindful that He is God—and we are not.

A healthy fear of God also improves the odds that we will live according to His design rather than doing only what we want to do. Our appropriate reverence for our holy God will help prevent us from choosing to participate in sinful behavior.

Be warned that involvement in sin will squelch your fear of God. You will unconsciously put aside what you know to be the truth. You will suppress your knowledge of Him and struggle even more to change your ways.

So fear God, serve Him, and know His blessing!

God is greatly to be feared in the assembly
    of the saints,
And to be held in reverence by all those
    around Him.
O Lord God of hosts,
Who is mighty like You, O Lord?

PSALM 89:7–8

You shall walk after the Lord your God and fear Him, and keep His commandments and obey His voice; you shall serve Him and hold fast to Him.

DEUTERONOMY 13:4

All nations whom You have made
Shall come and worship before You, O Lord,
And shall glorify Your name.
For You are great, and do wondrous things;
You alone are God.

PSALM 86:9–10

Fear the LORD, and serve Him in truth with all your heart; for consider what great things He has done for you.

1 SAMUEL 12:24

ONE PURPOSE

Jesus, God's only Son, came into the world with one purpose, and that was to die for our sins and save us from the eternal consequences of those sins. Jesus devoted His life to this ultimate act of service to humankind.

What is the purpose God created you for? How can you find out? Ask God for guidance, ask friends for feedback on your strengths and weaknesses, list ways your life can honor God and reflect His love. Examine your talents and desires for clues about how God wants to use you.

Seek the Lord, and He will make your purpose clear.

And let the beauty of the Lord our God be
    upon us,
And establish the work of our hands for us;
Yes, establish the work of our hands.

PSALM 90:17

It is God who works in you both to will and
to do for His good pleasure.

PHILIPPIANS 2:13

We are His workmanship, created in Christ
Jesus for good works, which God prepared
beforehand that we should walk in them.

EPHESIANS 2:10

"Indeed for this purpose I have raised you up,
that I may show My power in you, and that
My name may be declared in all the earth."

EXODUS 9:16

THE BLESSING OF THE HOLY SPIRIT

After Jesus defeated death by dying on the cross and rising from the dead, He sent His followers the gift of His Spirit. The Holy Spirit lives within each of us Jesus-followers today as well, and the Spirit guides our decisions and directs our lives. The Spirit transforms us and makes us more like Jesus.

The Holy Spirit is known as the Helper, the Teacher, the Comforter—and He prays for you at God's throne! So walk in the Spirit. Open yourself to His help, His teaching, and His comfort.

As you walk in the Spirit, you will be blessed.

The Spirit also helps in our weaknesses. For we do not know what we should pray for as we ought, but the Spirit Himself makes intercession for us with groanings which cannot be uttered.

ROMANS 8:26

"When He, the Spirit of truth, has come, He will guide you into all truth; for He will not speak on His own authority, but whatever He hears He will speak; and He will tell you things to come."

JOHN 16:13

The Spirit Himself bears witness with our spirit that we are children of God, and if children, then heirs—heirs of God and joint heirs with Christ, if indeed we suffer with Him, that we may also be glorified together.

ROMANS 8:16–17

Now may the God of hope fill you with all joy and peace in believing, that you may abound in hope by the power of the Holy Spirit.

ROMANS 15:13

AVAILABLE 24/7

God promises to give us wisdom when we ask Him, yet much of His wisdom is accessible to us 24/7. Just open the Bible!

The more we read and study Scripture, the more we meditate on and memorize God's Word, the wiser we will become. The Word teaches us how to honor God, and those guidelines are for our good. Even the hard stretches of life will go better when we follow God's instructions and learn from the flesh-and-blood examples of faith found in Scripture.

Furthermore, the Bible offers a road map for a rich and significant life in Christ. After all, God created us to live in communion with Him. Remember that no matter where you are or what you face, His wisdom is accessible 24/7. Let His Word be "a lamp to [your] feet and a light to [your] path" (Psalm 119:105).

How sweet are Your words to my taste,
Sweeter than honey to my mouth!
Through Your precepts I get understanding.

PSALM 119:103–104

Receive my instruction, and not silver,
And knowledge rather than choice gold;
For wisdom is better than rubies,
And all the things one may desire cannot be
    compared with her.

PROVERBS 8:10–11

Your righteousness is an everlasting
    righteousness,
And Your law is truth. . . .
Your commandments are my delights.
The righteousness of Your testimonies is
    everlasting;
Give me understanding, and I shall live.

PSALM 119:142, 144

UNDER ENEMY ATTACK

In His Word, God warns us that our enemy will attack: "Be sober, be vigilant; because your adversary the devil walks about like a roaring lion, seeking whom he may devour" (1 Peter 5:8). Therefore He tells us to "[take] the shield of faith with which [we] will be able to quench all the fiery darts of the wicked one" (Ephesians 6:16). By the power of His Spirit, God enables us to recognize the Enemy's deceitful words.

We need both the shield and the Spirit, for we live in a world at war. Satan's darkness, despair, and hate still fight against the truth, the light, the hope, and the love of God. In His crucifixion and resurrection, Jesus proved victorious: this sinless Lamb of God defeated death by rising into glorious life. Although he has lost, Satan is always battling against God's people.

Is your shield of faith in place? Are you relying on God's Spirit for help navigating life while under enemy attack?

Put on the whole armor of God, that you may be able to stand against the wiles of the devil.

EPHESIANS 6:11

We do not wrestle against flesh and blood, but against principalities, against powers, against the rulers of the darkness of this age, against spiritual hosts of wickedness in the heavenly places.

EPHESIANS 6:12

The LORD is my rock and my fortress and my
    deliverer;
My God, my strength, in whom I will trust;
My shield and the horn of my salvation, my
    stronghold.
I will call upon the LORD, who is worthy to be
    praised;
So shall I be saved from my enemies.

PSALM 18:2–3

Yea, though I walk through the valley of the
    shadow of death,
I will fear no evil;
For You are with me;
Your rod and Your staff, they comfort me.

PSALM 23:4

GOD'S EMPOWERING PRESENCE

When we choose first thing in the morning to walk with God throughout the day, however ordinary and uneventful we expect it to be, we can trust Him to guide our thoughts and actions.

God will, for instance, enable us to think about "whatever things are true, whatever things are noble, whatever things are just, whatever things are pure, whatever things are lovely, whatever things are of good report" (Philippians 4:8). Our ever-present Lord will also inspire us to act with Christlike love, turning the other cheek, giving away our cloak as well as our tunic, and praying for our enemies (Matthew 5:39–40, 44).

May we make it a practice to pray when we have a decision to make, to speak and act as

Jesus wants us to, and to be aware every waking hour of His empowering presence with us.

You will show me the path of life;
In Your presence is fullness of joy;
At Your right hand are pleasures forevermore.

PSALM 16:11

The LORD is on my side;
I will not fear.

PSALM 118:6

I have set the LORD always before me;
Because He is at my right hand I shall not be
    moved.
Therefore my heart is glad, and my glory
    rejoices;
My flesh also will rest in hope.

PSALM 16:8–9

Those who trust in the Lord
Are like Mount Zion,
Which cannot be moved, but abides forever.
As the mountains surround Jerusalem,
So the Lord surrounds His people
From this time forth and forever.

PSALM 125:1–2

Be strong and of good courage, do not fear
nor be afraid of them; for the Lord your God,
He is the One who goes with you. He will not
leave you nor forsake you.

DEUTERONOMY 31:6

DROP DOUBT

D oubt is the devil's tool—and he uses it very effectively and all too often.

For some believers, the distance between head and heart seems unbridgeable. Their heads contain a lot of knowledge about God. They intellectually understand and accept what they have learned from Scripture as truth. But their hearts don't always keep up.

Then, with an unexpected loss or crushing disappointment, the heart may cry out in pain. Suddenly the mind may not be so certain that it had fully or correctly understood who God is. Or maybe, because of a rough childhood, they have a solid head knowledge of God's love and confidence in His love for others, but no heartfelt certainty about God's love for them.

You are a child of God. Ask Him to help you drop doubt.

Lord, I believe; help my unbelief!

MARK 9:24

Jesus said to him, "Thomas, because you have seen Me, you have believed. Blessed are those who have not seen and yet have believed."

JOHN 20:29

Truly Jesus did many other signs in the presence of His disciples, which are not written in this book; but these are written that you may believe that Jesus is the Christ, the Son of God, and that believing you may have life in His name.

JOHN 20:30–31

Let him [who lacks wisdom] ask in faith, with no doubting, for he who doubts is like a wave of the sea driven and tossed by the wind.

JAMES 1:6

And immediately Jesus stretched out His hand and caught him, and said to him, "O you of little faith, why did you doubt?" And when they got into the boat, the wind ceased. Then those who were in the boat came and worshiped Him, saying, "Truly You are the Son of God."

MATTHEW 14:31–33

HEAVEN AHEAD!

E very human being will live eternally. Some of us will live forever with God in the glory of heaven. Others, however, will live for eternity in the dark separation from God they chose when they walked this earth. If you have committed your heart and your life to Jesus, heaven is ready for you.

Consider what a voice from heaven has said: "God will wipe away every tear from their eyes; there shall be no more death, nor sorrow, nor crying. There shall be no more pain" (Revelation 21:4). Our eternal life with Christ began the minute we named Him our Savior, and that eternal life will one day—and forever—be glorious.

When you're weary of earth, look toward the future and remember: heaven ahead!

Blessed be the God and Father of our
Lord Jesus Christ, who according to His
abundant mercy has begotten us again to
a living hope through the resurrection of
Jesus Christ from the dead, to an inheritance
incorruptible and undefiled and that does
not fade away, reserved in heaven for you.

1 PETER 1:3-5

In Him you also trusted, after you heard the
word of truth, the gospel of your salvation;
in whom also, having believed, you were
sealed with the Holy Spirit of promise, who
is the guarantee of our inheritance until the
redemption of the purchased possession, to
the praise of His glory.

EPHESIANS 1:13-14

The wages of sin is death, but the gift of God is eternal life in Christ Jesus our Lord.

ROMANS 6:23

He who sat on the throne said, "Behold, I make all things new." . . . And He said to me, "It is done! I am the Alpha and the Omega, the Beginning and the End. I will give of the fountain of the water of life freely to him who thirsts. He who overcomes shall inherit all things, and I will be his God and he shall be My son."

REVELATION 21:5-7

YOUR PERFECT PARENT

A re not five sparrows sold for two copper coins?" Jesus asked the crowd. "And not one of them is forgotten before God. But the very hairs of your head are all numbered. Do not fear therefore; you are of more value than many sparrows" (Luke 12:6–7).

Your Father God knows your heart, your concerns, and your responsibilities as well as the number of hairs on your head. He sees, He is aware, and He cares—but the enemy of your soul wants you to think otherwise. When you have those toxic thoughts, it's time to speak out loud the truth that you are a child of God, a child of the King of kings. The apostle John put it this way: "Behold what manner of love the Father has bestowed on us, that we should be called children of God!" (1 John 3:1).

As the Lord's child, you can absolutely rely

upon His goodness. After all, He is your perfect Parent.

I have been young, and now am old;
Yet I have not seen the righteous forsaken,
Nor his descendants begging bread.
He is ever merciful, and lends;
And his descendants are blessed.

PSALM 37:25–26

When my father and my mother forsake me,
Then the LORD will take care of me.

PSALM 27:10

"I will be a Father to you,
And you shall be My sons and daughters,"
Says the LORD Almighty.

2 CORINTHIANS 6:18

GOD-GIVEN STRENGTH

Jesus asked His disciples to stay awake and pray for Him while He begged His Father to let the cup of suffering pass (Mark 14:32–42). Three times Jesus returned and found the disciples asleep. But God strengthened His Son to face His critical moment. He'll do the same for you.

God promises to give us the perseverance we need to handle life's most difficult moments. In Scripture God promises to jumpstart our strength so we'll persevere when all we want to do is drop.

As you fulfill God's plans for you, you will face times when your strength threatens to fail. Ask Him to empower you to carry on. He will! He guarantees it in His Word: "As your days, so shall your strength be" (Deuteronomy 33:25).

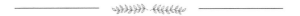

[The Lord God] gives power to the weak,
And to those who have no might He
increases strength.

ISAIAH 40:29

I know that the Lord saves His anointed;
He will answer him from His holy heaven
With the saving strength of His right hand.

PSALM 20:6

Do not cast away your confidence, which
has great reward. For you have need of
endurance, so that after you have done the
will of God, you may receive the promise.

HEBREWS 10:35–36

THE WHOLE WORD OF GOD

The book of Proverbs offers commentary on the value of wisdom as well as directives for many aspects of life. But wisdom is actually found throughout the Word of God—from Genesis 1 through Revelation 22—and when we choose to make the Bible part of our everyday lives, we learn and internalize that wisdom.

Are you taking hold of God's Word? Whenever you open its pages, do you ask the Spirit to show you what God has for you? Today, pray with the psalmist, "Teach me Your way, O LORD, and lead me in a smooth path" (Psalm 27:11). Then read and receive whatever God reveals to you through His Word.

Let the word of Christ dwell in you richly in all wisdom, teaching and admonishing one another in psalms and hymns and spiritual songs, singing with grace in your hearts to the Lord.

COLOSSIANS 3:16

The LORD gives wisdom;
From His mouth come knowledge and
    understanding;
He stores up sound wisdom for the upright;
He is a shield to those who walk uprightly.

PROVERBS 2:6-7

I have taught you in the way of wisdom;

I have led you in right paths.

When you walk, your steps will not be
   hindered,

And when you run, you will not stumble.

Take firm hold of instruction, do not let go;

Keep her, for she is your life.

PROVERBS 4:11–13

All Scripture is given by inspiration of God,
and is profitable for doctrine, for reproof, for
correction, for instruction in righteousness,
that the man of God may be complete, thoroughly equipped for every good work.

2 TIMOTHY 3:16–17

TODAY'S HEROES

Who comes to mind when you read the word *hero*? Do you think of anyone alive today? What character traits do you consider heroic? What kind of accomplishments?

Perhaps you're thinking we're a little low on heroes today, at least the kind who make the news. What about teachers and professors who respond to God's call to teach despite low pay and, in the world's eyes, less status? What about coaches who pour time and inspiration into athletes, building not only better competitors but better individuals?

Our age may not be short of heroes. They just may be low-profile. Whenever you have an opportunity to act courageously, ask God to give you strength. Our world needs people who will stand tall in their relationship with the Almighty, stand firm in the truth He has taught them, and stay strong in their commitment to serving Him and others. If you overcome fear to do these things, you are truly a hero.

"Be strong and of good courage; do not be afraid, nor be dismayed, for the LORD your God is with you wherever you go."

JOSHUA 1:9

Whatever you do, do it heartily, as to the Lord and not to men.

COLOSSIANS 3:23

Immediately Jesus spoke to them, saying, "Be of good cheer! It is I; do not be afraid."

MATTHEW 14:27

So now, brethren, I commend you to God and to the word of His grace, which is able to build you up and give you an inheritance among all those who are sanctified.

ACTS 20:32

And God has appointed these in the church: first apostles, second prophets, third teachers, after that miracles, then gifts of healings, helps, administrations, varieties of tongues.

1 CORINTHIANS 12:28

GOD'S COMFORTING PRESENCE AND PROVISION

Maybe you've never looked at these passages side by side. In 2 Corinthians 11, Paul recalled beatings, a stoning, three shipwrecks, and such perils as robbers, the wilderness, the sea, and hunger (vv. 23–27). In Philippians, this same Paul wrote, "I have learned in whatever state I am, to be content" (4:11). Two things contributed to Paul's contentment despite his circumstances.

First, Paul knew the reality of God's strength when he was weak (2 Corinthians 12:10). When Paul received supernatural power, he experienced God's presence as well as His acceptance and love.

Second, Paul maintained a big-picture perspective. God had taken care of his greatest need by giving His Son as Savior, so Paul could be sure He would take care of every other need he had.

You can be sure of God's comforting presence and provision as well! What concern can you take to Him today in exchange for His help?

In the multitude of my anxieties within me,
Your comforts delight my soul.

PSALM 94:19

He who did not spare His own Son, but delivered Him up for us all, how shall He not with Him also freely give us all things?

ROMANS 8:32

You, who have shown me great and severe
    troubles,
Shall revive me again,
And bring me up again from the depths of
    the earth. . . .
My lips shall greatly rejoice when I sing
    to You,
And my soul, which You have redeemed.

PSALM 71:20, 23

And my God shall supply all your need
according to His riches in glory by Christ
Jesus.

PHILIPPIANS 4:19

ILLOGICAL AND SUPERNATURAL

Maybe you experienced nervousness or even borderline panic when you took your driving test, before you went into a big exam, or during your first job interview. Or maybe you experienced the peace that God gives, the peace the apostle Paul spoke over fellow believers: "Grace to you and peace from God our Father and the Lord Jesus Christ" (2 Corinthians 1:2).

Such peace is evidence that the Holy Spirit dwells within you (Galatians 5:22), and that calmness comes as you trust God with life's difficult circumstances and complete unknowns. When money is tight or the deadline looms or the doctor hasn't called with the lab results, draw near to God, pray, take deep breaths, read Scripture, ask Him for the gift of His comfort, and thank Him when He gives it. The illogical experience of supernatural peace in stressful times is God's grace in you.

Let the peace of God rule in your hearts, to which also you were called in one body; and be thankful.

COLOSSIANS 3:15

"Peace I leave with you, My peace I give to you; not as the world gives do I give to you. Let not your heart be troubled, neither let it be afraid."

JOHN 14:27

Those who live according to the flesh set
their minds on the things of the flesh, but
those who live according to the Spirit,
the things of the Spirit. For to be carnally
minded is death, but to be spiritually minded
is life and peace.

ROMANS 8:5-6

Depart from evil and do good;
Seek peace and pursue it.

PSALM 34:14

THE GIFT OF GOD'S WORD

Treasure chest. Road map. Instruction manual. Mirror. Compass. Flashlight. Food for life. Declaration of truth. Love letter.

This list offers only partial descriptions of God's Word and its multifaceted role in our lives. As we read the Bible, we come to understand our sin. We learn that God sent His Son, Jesus, to take on Himself the death penalty that we deserve for our sin. We gain access to God's wisdom. We find comfort for our wounded souls and broken spirits. We hear teachings about how to live, and we watch how Jesus loved God and others. We find words of praise we can echo, and we find hope for the future, for our eternal future.

For these reasons and more, may God grow in you a greater hunger for the gift of His Word and, each time you open its pages, a keen awareness of what He has to say, especially to you.

"It is written, 'Man shall not live by bread alone, but by every word that proceeds from the mouth of God.'"

MATTHEW 4:4

The word of God is living and powerful, and sharper than any two-edged sword, piercing even to the division of soul and spirit, and of joints and marrow, and is a discerner of the thoughts and intents of the heart.

HEBREWS 4:12

"Heaven and earth will pass away, but My words will by no means pass away."

LUKE 21:33

Your word I have hidden in my heart,
That I might not sin against You.
Blessed are You, O LORD!
Teach me Your statutes. . . .
I will not forget Your word.

PSALM 119:11–12, 16